A Call to Redemption:

God's Road to Salvation

DOROTHY NELSON

A Call to Redemption:
GOD'S ROAD TO SALVATION

A Call to Redemption: God's Road to Salvation

Dorothy A. Nelson

Copyright © 2017 by Dorothy A. Nelson

Published by Scribe
Publications, Inc.
404-919-1931

http://www.scribepublicationsinc.com

Cover Design by Chris Middleton

All rights reserved. This book or parts thereof may not be reproduced in any form, stored in a retrieval system, or transmitted in any form by any means - electronic, mechanical, photocopy, recording, or otherwise - without prior written permission of the publisher, except as provided by United States of America copyright law.

Unless otherwise identified, scripture quotations are from the Holy Bible King James Version, Cambridge, 1769. Used by permission. All rights reserved.

Scripture quotations marked AMP are taken from the Amplified Bible, Copyright (c) 1954, 1958, 1962, 1964, 1965, 1987 by The Lockman Foundation. Used by permission.

Scripture quotations noted NLT are from the Holy Bible, New Living Translation. Copyright (c) 1996 and 2004. Used by permission of Tyndale House Publishers, Wheaton, Illinois. 60190. All rights reserved.

Scripture quotations noted MSG are from *The Message.* Copyright © 1993, 1994, 1995, 1996, 2000, 2001, 2002. Used by permission of NavPress Publishing Group.

Scripture quotations noted TLB are from The Living Bible copyright © 1971 by Tyndale House Foundation. Used by permission of Tyndale House Publishers Inc., Carol Stream, Illinois 60188. All rights reserved.

Scripture quotations noted (ESV) are from English Standard Version®, copyright © 2001 by Crossway, a publishing ministry of Good News Publishers. ESV® Text Edition: 2011. The ESV® text has been reproduced in cooperation with and by permission of Good News Publishers.

Scripture quotations noted (WNT) are from Weymouth New Testament, copyright © Richard Francis Weymouth 1903.

Any name referencing satan will not be given the respect of capitalization, even at the risk of improper sentence structure.

ISBN-13: 978-0-9967824-3-2

Library of Congress Control Number: 2017947392

Printed in the United States of America.

Table of Contents

Acknowledgements 8
Foreword..9
Introduction 11
Chapter One: Back to the Basics..17
Chapter Two: God's Plan of Salvation 38
Chapter Three: Repent and Turn to the Lord! 46
Chapter Four: The Valley of Decision 56
Salvation Confession 74
About the Author 77

Acknowledgements

First and foremost, special thanks goes to my Lord and Savior Jesus Christ for empowering me and anointing me to write this wonderful book in efforts to empower the body of Christ to reach the lost with effective soul witnessing. To God be all the glory!

Thanks and appreciation goes out to my dream team who, through the hands of God, works wonders to make me sound good with great editorial skills and look good with beautifully designed book covers.

Foreword

As the fourth oldest child and former armor bearer of Apostle Dorothy Nelson, I have nearly 40 years of up close and personal experiences of her life both publicly and privately. Without a doubt, she has been called to share the Gospel to the nations. I've watched and at times joined in with her as she labored with many souls. After more than 40 years in the ministry, her passion to win the lost has waxed even greater.

From the streets of Chicago to the small villages in East Africa, Apostle Nelson's message remains resoundingly clear....JESUS SAVES and God's plan of redemption is available to all who will call on the name of the Lord. She is equally impassioned about equipping the body of Christ with the needed tools to be effective soul winners. Since her days of street witnessing on the west side of Chicago, she has seen and encountered a great deal. These life experiences have helped to shape the message to those of us who walk the path that she's blazed in ministry.

In the pages of this impactful book, your heart will be set ablaze with the foundational truths of God's Word concerning winning the lost. Through this book, a revelation of His love and impartation of His wisdom will be experienced. As you read, you will see God's desire for each of us to be ministers of reconciliation to those who are seeking Him for salvation. Allow God to tenderize your heart and sensitize your ear to hear the cries of those who are in desperate need of the Savior.

Faithfully fulfilling the call,

Charity A. Morris

Introduction

Shhhh....Quiet yourselves. Can you hear it? Do you feel it....*the torturous cries of the lost.* They are wandering back and forth looking for answers. They are in desperate search for truth. They are in dire need of real power. THEY ARE HUNGRY FOR AUTHENTIC CHANGE! It's time to answer the call.

Romans 8:19 (WNT) - *For all creation, gazing eagerly as if with outstretched neck, is waiting and longing to see the manifestation of the sons of God.*

God is calling for those who are willing to go out into His vineyard and witness to the lost souls for this is the time and the season for all of the lost souls to come into God's Kingdom. Now, more than ever, are you willing to obey God's call when He bids you to work in the vineyard? Jesus gave us a prophetic commission to go into the world and preach the gospel to every creature, according to St. Mark 16: 15-20:

"Go ye into all the world, and preach the gospel to every creature. He that believeth and is baptized shall be saved; but he that believeth not shall be damned. And these signs shall follow them that believe; in my name shall they cast out devils; they shall speak with new tongues; they shall take up serpents; and if they drink any deadly things, it shall not hurt them; they shall lay hands on the sick, and they shall recover. So then after the Lord had spoken unto them, he was received up into Heaven, and sat on the right hand of God. And they went forth, and preached everywhere, the Lord working with them, and confirming the Word with signs following."

Are you willing to stand in the gap for the lost souls? My brothers and sisters, if we are not ready, God will raise up someone else who is willing and ready! The world is crying out for release and freedom from the bondages of sin! There is a clarion called against sin, like in the days of old. Similar to in the time and likeness of John the Baptist, I believe that God will raise up those who are not afraid to cry out loud and spare not against the sins of our nation. John the Baptist told the people in the marketplaces and streets, *"Repent, for the Kingdom of God is at hand!"* (St. Matthew 3:1-2). He cried out against adultery, corrupt politicians, unfair wages and unjust laws. How much more should we stand and cry out against unjust laws and their conditions? We, as God's representatives, should take a Godly stand against the sins of our world and nation. God is raising these modern-day John the Baptists who will not be intimidated to preach and cry out against abortion clinics, drug houses, whore houses, sex slavery, alcoholism, domestic abuse, homosexuality and all other forms of sins and prejudices.

Shouldn't we be God's Ambassadors for the body of Christ? Be as John the Baptist, who was called by God and radically anointed to go into all the world. God is waiting for us to go out and compel them to come. He has already given us permission and has told us what to do, where to go and how to do it. So, my brothers and sisters the time is N-O-W! Do you see the violence in our land, the sickness, diseases and murderers of fathers and mothers and children? Do you see the chiasmic divide of races and ethnicities? Do you see how the enemy is pitting citizens against police and politicians? Do you feel the civil unrest in society? The Word tells us that *where sins abound grace much more abounds* (Romans 5:20).

Although the world is becoming more and more evil by the day, God has given us divine protection to fulfill his mandate.

> **Psalm 118:6** - *The LORD is on my side; I will not fear: what can man do unto me?*

> **Hebrews 13:5** *(AMP) - for He [God] Himself has said, I will not in any way fail you nor give you up nor leave you without support. [I will] not, [I will] not, [I will] not in any degree leave you helpless nor forsake nor let [you] down (relax My hold on you)! Assuredly not!]*

> **Luke 10:19** - *Behold, I give unto you power to tread on serpents and scorpions, and over all the power of the enemy: and nothing shall by any means hurt you.*

Dorothy A. Nelson

Isaiah 41:10 – *So do not fear, for I am with you, do not be dismayed, for I am your God. I will strengthen you and help you. I will uphold you with My righteous right hand*

Jesus commanded "Go!" Are you ready to go? I'm telling you, there are people who are ready to hear the gospel, the good news, and ready to be set free in spirit, soul and body!

As you read, allow the Spirit of God to impart into your heart His passion for souls. Let the love of Jesus Christ compel you to reach the heirs of salvation. I pray that this book on salvation and soul-winning will be a great resource in helping you to become a great witness for the Lord Jesus Christ. It will serve as a valuable tool for you to use and as a salvation reference for scripture. It will also help to enlighten and enhance your spiritual knowledge in the word of God. This booklet will help bring you to a place with God to give you the courage and boldness you will need to be at your best when venturing in your neighborhoods, communities, market places, cities and regions. Wherever this gospel may lead you to go, by God's grace, you will be equipped by the Spirit of God. So I say to you, "Go in Jesus' name and be blessed because God will reward you for your faithfulness in winning souls for His Kingdom!"

Chapter One:
Back to the Basics

In Matthew 4, Jesus' first words to Simon Peter and his brother Andrew was about winning souls. He made a promise to them that if they followed Him, he would teach them how to win souls.

> ***Matthew 4:18-19*** *(TLB) –* *18 One day as he was walking along the beach beside the Lake of Galilee, he saw two brothers—Simon, also called Peter, and Andrew—out in a boat[a] fishing with a net, for they were commercial fishermen. 19 Jesus called out, "Come along with me and I will show you how to fish for the souls of men!"*

To reemphasize His first words during His first encounter with the disciples, His final words to all the disciples was to go out and replicate themselves.

> ***Matthew 28:19*** *(TLB) – Therefore go and make disciples in all the nations, baptizing them into the name of the Father and of the Son and of the Holy Spirit*

As you can see, Jesus' first and last concern was about saving souls. Everything He did in between those two moments in time pointed right back to His primary purpose, redeeming man and restoring right relationship. All the miracles, teachings, prophecies point back to the redemptive plan of Christ.

If we are to follow in Jesus' footsteps, then everything we do should point people back to the Father. The preaching is great, the teaching is wonder, miracles and healings are exciting but are people being drawn to the Father or to you? Is your message Christ-centered or self-centered?

The body of Christ has focused so much on the sensational that we've left the essential. Let's get back to making the main thing the main thing.

Here are some very important pointers concerning witnessing and street preaching. First, although you may not be called to the five-fold ministry (apostle, prophet, pastor, evangelist, teacher), we are ALL called to be ministers of reconciliation: *And all things are of God, who hath reconciled us to himself by Jesus Christ, and hath given to us the ministry of reconciliation (2 Corinthians 5:18).* Will you lead every person you encounter to the Lord? Maybe not, but just make sure they have an encounter with Jesus when you do talk with them.

Second, you must love and have great compassion for souls. Ask God for a heart that is tender towards the lost. Pray this prayer: *Father, sensitize my heart to feel what you feel, see what you see and hear the cries of the lost.*

Third, ask God to anoint to reach the lost souls. Pray this prayer: *Father, make me a magnet for souls. Let the anointing draw them to me and me to them so that they may have an encounter with Your love, grace and peace.*

Before you venture out to the streets to witness, your next step is to develop a close personal relationship with the Lord through prayer and reading His Word! This is now your time of preparation and studying of God's Word so that you may be equipped to handle the Word of God in its' entirety. This time will be devoted to building up your knowledge and faith in God and it will also serve to build confidence in you, as well as in God.

Now there is a difference between street witnessing and street preaching. Street witnessing is when one goes from house to house, neighborhood to neighborhood spreading the gospel of Jesus Christ. This is done through tracts, pamphlets, and other forms of literature that talks about God's plan for salvation. In many cases, you will even leave gospel materials and/or literature on door knobs, fences or inside of doors. In doing this people, may receive the opportunity to hear and read the good news! Understand sometimes you may get those individuals who reject you and your literature. If so, just kindly hand them the gospel tracts and tell them to have a nice day. Further in the book, I will discuss in more detail street witnessing.

Street preaching involves one who declares and proclaims the gospel in the streets of a community. A street preacher is one who has a more visible form of preaching than a street witness. Street preachers are assigned to preach on the street corners or wherever the Spirit of God leads them. Some preach in the inner-city areas and in subways, trains and buses. In addition, many street preachers choose to use a microphone and small amplifier, which allows their voice to carry and the message of salvation is amplified to be heard more strongly by a greater number of people. Street preachers may use different spots on different corners to stand and preach the gospel. Some street preachers' assignments may be to preach the gospel from morning until night on one corner until God releases them. That is why there must be a call from God for this particular assignment. When a street preacher obeys the will of God and preaches to the unsaved, they will be looked down upon by many of the individuals they are preaching to. They will be hated. They will be shunned and ignored. They will be mocked and laughed at by both nonbelievers and sadly by some of our very own brethren in Christ. They will face these actions by the very people who they are driven to reach on the streets.

In my day, I have seen many individuals who have preached on subways, trains and especially in various inner city areas with a bull horn. Believe me, there were many people who would pass by these preachers and try to ignore them by crossing over to the other side of the street. Many individuals would frown when they would pass by these street preachers. However, I thought at that time, that this was very strange, but good. I was not saved during those days, but years later, I have embraced it and truly love street preaching and witnessing.

Street preachers are not ashamed to stand and preach the Gospel of the Kingdom. They are unashamed and their assignment is to get the gospel out whether you like or accept it or not. They are commissioned by God to preach the acceptable year of the Lord to a dying world. So, you see it takes something special to stand on the street corners while being ignored and talked about. Yet, these street preachers continue to preach the gospel. Their job is preaching, even if no one responds, these individuals should and prayerfully will continue to preach!

If God has placed a passion and burning desire in your soul to street preach, please do not allow your zeal to make you stumble past compliance with rules and regulations. With your zeal, make sure you are following the laws of the land. Some cities require street preachers to obtain preaching licenses, which will allow them to preach on city streets and other public places. It is not like 40 years ago, when an individual could go anywhere in whatever city o and preach. Now the enemy is making it harder for street preachers. Even with the enemy's advances, God always shows His people favor to get the Word out to the lost. Amen!

Street preaching now days are not as common as it used to be; it seems like they are becoming a rare species. However, I believe that God is raising up the individuals who embody the spirit of John the Baptist to cry out loud against sins in the market places, street corners, drug houses, whore houses and abortion clinics. God is raising an army of people who will be bold enough to cry out loud against the adulterers and fornicators and crooked politicians and unjust laws. He is preparing a remnant of Believers who are quick to obey His voice in this season to preach His Gospel on the street corners. Beloved, these days are coming and they are coming soon! Get ready to see and hear God's street preachers on every street corner. I loose it to be so in Jesus' mighty name! Amen.

Street witnessing flows in the same vein as street preaching. As with street preaching, you must have a love for street witnessing because your love for this will be challenged by those individuals to whom you are witnessing. They may make fun of you and call you out your name, and some may even refuse to hear what you have to say. That comes with the territory. Don't allow the negativity to make you lose your focus on your true assignment of reaching and winning lost souls to the Kingdom. Remember you have been properly prepared for this special assignment.

My very first witnessing assignment was at a very prominent hospital in Chicago, Illinois. You can say that this particular instance was my "test of obedience" to God and to His will, my test to see if I were truly willing to follow His instruction. I vividly remember this. After we had finished our morning breakfast with the family, the Spirit of the Lord came upon me and spoke to me and said, "I want you to go to Cook County Hospital!" I thought to myself "What are you saying?" Oh, and by the way, I was 5 1/2 months pregnant and didn't know a single person who was involved with this hospital at that time. Once again, the voice of God spoke to me in a very strong manner and His voice seemed as if it was like a multitude of ocean waves rushing into my soul. His voice seemed as if it were under deep layers of water beneath the sea. It pierced through my soul. It was like my bones were affected by it. My whole body shook at the sound of His voice! I thought to myself, "Wow! What POWER!" At that very moment I fell over on my bed and said "Yes...yes I will go!" I was crying and trembling because of the power of God's voice. Beloved, I could not say anything but, "Yes." I then proceeded to go downstairs and tell my husband, and as I continued to cry, my husband David knew that I had heard the voice of God and had a spiritual encounter with Him, and that His presence was still very strong upon me.

All I did from that moment forward was obey God. Not knowing where I was going to go upon arrival at the hospital, God was directing me as I was driving and crying. The Lord was making a divine way for me before I had even arrived. It was approximately a fifty-minute drive for me to get to the hospital and once I arrived at the hospital complex, the Lord had worked everything out for me. As I checked myself in at the hospital guard desk, I didn't even have to say a single word. The guard immediately handed me a guest pass with no questions asked. I then proceeded to the elevator and headed to the third floor. On the third floor, there were patients who had gunshot wounds and other traumatic injuries. These patients were stable but in serious condition. As I walked down the hallway of the ward, I saw many patients with severe head injuries and major leg injuries, including amputations. I wasn't sure what to do. As I continued to walk God, spoke to me in a soft voice and said, "Stop here." Now, this particular ward was for men. God instructed me to lay hands on and pray for those who had been injured. I ministered to about 5 souls that day before my assignment was over.

There was one individual who was a Muslim. This individual tried to test me on what I knew about God. He spoke of his knowledge which he stated he gleaned from reading the Koran. The Koran is Allah's holy word revealed to Muhammad through various supposed divine revelations. After my conversation with this individual, he accepted prayer from me! It was evident that the power of God moved upon every single person I ministered to that day. They each received the word of God due to my obedience to Him.

I didn't know where I was to go or who I was supposed to speak to, but the Holy Ghost lead me to the men who needed to hear the word of God and they all received it from the Lord!

As you see, when you are led by God, He will make a way for you! Beloved, when I left the hospital and headed home, I felt like a million bucks. I felt so unbelievably good! Just to obey God and to fulfill His will is so enriching to the soul. God gets all the glory! All God is seeking is to see if you will obey His will.

From that moment forward, I have been ministering in the streets. I receive such joy from street witnessing because I truly feel the heart of God is to have souls come into the Kingdom. Amen. It doesn't matter if you are pregnant or a senior, are you willing to say yes to His will?

Throughout my ministry and still to this day, I have a great love and passion for street ministry. Now I speak to and instruct those who have a desire to be a street witness for the Lord. You must be prepared to go the distance if you plan on being effective in ministering to the hurting, to the doubting and to the unbelieving.

What do you say to the person who thinks, "I don't need God right now because I am having too much fun!"? What do you say to the pastor who walked away from his ministry after his 5-year-old son was murdered in the streets of Detroit? What do you say to the former first lady of a prominent church who is now practicing Buddhism after her philandering preacher husband repeatedly cheated on her with men and women and had a love child with one of the women? What do you say to the parents who watched two of their children die of leukemia? Be ready, Beloved! You will meet former pastors, leaders and others who have lost their faith and their way; they have compromised and allowed their relationship with God.

For whatever reason these individuals give you when you come across them while witnessing, you will just have to stop for a moment and listen to what they have to say. Do not try to prove how deep you are in the Word. Truth be told, these individuals may know more than you. Remember, they once served as pastors and ministry leaders themselves. Backsliders will always know God's Word; whether they live it or not, it will never leave them.

It is important to just listen to them and you will locate the place where they are coming from and then God will reveal to you how to minister to their pain and hurt. Always be kind and understanding; always show compassion because there is always a story behind each situation.

During my times of street witnessing, I met pastors, prophets and ministers who have lost everything including their families. The pressure of their loss was too much to handle. They thought God had left them and allowed the enemy to destroy all that they had accomplished. Some had faced sickness, financial ruin, and death of loved ones and even loss of their ministry and/or their churches. As I have previously stated, you must just listen and God will give you what you need to say. When you say these words, God has given to you, they will bring comfort and peace. Say this prayer: Lord, let my words be seasoned with love, healing and deliverance. Amen.

The former pastor and ministry leader is no different than the person who's never received Jesus Christ as their Lord and Savior. They need to be loved and encouraged. The pastor who walked away from it all just need to hear that anyone can come back to the Lord Jesus Christ and that He is waiting for them! Praise God! He is a restorer of the brokenhearted.

Now that I have discussed with you the difference between street preaching and street witnessing and also how God uses them both to get the message of the Kingdom out to the hurting world, whichever ministry God has called you to, please make sure you are ready and go forth! When you do, God's anointing will rest upon you to get His job done all for His glory.

A Call to Redemption

During your time of preparation, make sure to read the Word, pray, fast and stay in constant fellowship with Him until your time of release. Amen! Beloved, when you do all of this, you will have a good head start and a strong foundation with God and His Word. For your willingness and obedience to God, He will reward you.

It is very important that, as a street witness, you make sure to have all your ministry material and literature with you for distribution. Also, never ever argue with the Word. Yes, you must be ready to give an answer and defend the faith but never, and I repeat NEVER argue. Likewise, it is perfectly okay to say you don't have the answer; sometimes that's the best answer instead of trying to make something up for the sake of having an "answer." There will be some days when you will be instructed to just hand out information (tracts, Bibles, flyers, etc.) and then keep it moving. Remember, *one plants, another waters but the Lord brings the increase* (1 Corinthians 3:6-7 paraphrase).

If someone stops you and presents you a specific question concerning the information package you have given them, be ready at that time to minister God's love and salvation to them and always make sure you minister according to God's Word. Your opinion, your theories, your intellect is not what's needed. Stick to the Word! When you do this, you will never go wrong.

Sometimes God will use you to give your testimony because your testimony is your true story of how God delivered you. Sometimes the best thing you can do is share the love of Jesus Christ by way of your story. God will use you differently at different times. As an example, God may allow you to approach a person like this, "Excuse me, may I share some good news with you?" Many times, just making this simple statement will open a door to conversation. At other times, God may have you approach an individual and start a conversation. You may even choose to pass out tracts. However you approach a passerby, the Word must be shared.

For those of you who have a strong desire to be an effective street witness, I have prepared some basic salvation scriptures which will help you as you minister. Please take full advantage of this information which will help you in becoming a better, more well-rounded witness for The Lord Jesus Christ. Always remember that God has not given us the spirit of fear, but of power, love and sound mind. Amen.

Beloved, I am not trying to scare you, but trying to help and adequately prepare you for your witnessing by equipping you to handle every situation that may come your way. Like I have said before, you must always be ready because the enemy will test you for what you know about God and yourself as well. The enemy's job is to stop and hinder the Word of God from advancing.

To each who desires to witness, make sure that you and your witness team stay focused on your assignment because the two of you balance each other out while you minister to the lost with the message of salvation. If you are ever in doubt, let your minister partner step in. Amen. Remember, it is all about the lost souls and never about us! Please always keep that mind when going out to street witness. Always go in pairs just as Jesus sent his disciples to witness two by two in every city with His blessing. Please share what you desire to do with your pastors and ministers and get their approval before going out. Make sure you never go out to witness without your pastor's blessing because you wouldn't want the devil to cause an onslaught against you and your assignment.

St. Matthew 10: 1-14

"And when He had called unto Him Twelve disciples, He gave them power against unclean spirit, to cast them out, and to heal all manner of sickness and all manner of disease. Now the names of the Twelve apostles are these: The First, Simon, who is called Peter, and Andrew his brother; James the Son of Zebedee, and John his brother; Philip, and Bartholomew; Thomas, and Matthew the Publican; James the Son of Al-phae-us and Leb-bae-us, whose surname was Thadd-dae-us; Simon the Ca-na-an-ite, and Judas Iscariot, who also betrayed him. These Twelve Jesus sent forth, and commanded them, saying, Go not into the way of the Gentiles, and into any city of the Samaritans enter ye not. But go rather to the lost sheep of the House of Israel. And as ye go, preach, saying, the Kingdom of Heaven is at hand. Heal the sick, cleanse the lepers, raise the dead, cast out devils; freely ye have received, freely give. Provide neither gold, nor silver, nor brass in your purses. Nor scrip for your journey, neither two coats, neither shoes, nor yet staves; for the workman is worthy of meat. An in whatsoever city or town ye shall enter, inquire who in it is worthy, and there abide till ye go thence. And when ye come into a house salute it. And if they house be worthy, let your peace come upon it, but if it be not worthy, let you peace return to you. And whosoever shall not received you, nor hear your words, when ye depart out of that house or city, shake off the dust of your feet."

A Call to Redemption

St. Matthew 9: 35-38

And Jesus went about all the cities and villages, teaching in their synagogues, and preaching the Gospel of the Kingdom, and healing every sickness and every disease among the people. But when he saw the multitudes, he was moved with compassion on them, because they fainted, and were scattered abroad, as sheep having no shepherd. Then saith he unto his disciples, the harvest truly is plenteous, but the laborers are few; pray ye therefore The Lord of the harvest, that he will send forth laborers into the harvest."

Soul winners, get ready, because these days are coming back! Stay at the feet of Jesus until He releases you into the market place. Signs and wonders shall follow you as you do as Jesus did when he obeyed His Father concerning souls.

Now do you see why it is necessary to obey the calling of God? People are falling, fainting and dying. God needs more disciples who are willing to go forth/ are you willing? If so, let's get ready now!

St. Luke 10: 16-23

"He that heareth you heareth me, and he that despiseth you despiseth me; and he that despiseth me despiseth him that sent me. And the seventy returned again with joy, saying, Lord, even the devils are subject unto us through Thy Name. And he said unto them, I beheld Satan as lightning fall from the Heaven. Behold, I give unto you power to tread on serpents and scorpions, and over all the power of the enemy; and nothing shall by any means hurt you. Notwithstanding in this rejoice, because your name is written in Heaven."

When we are in the will of God and doing the work of the Kingdom by ministering to lost souls, the enemy cannot harm us. When we go in the Spirit of His might, The Lord anoints us with His power, through the Holy Ghost. Amen. As you go forth, go in His power and put on the whole armor according to **Ephesians 6:10-18**:

"Finally, my brethren, be strong in The Lord, and in the power of His might. Put on the whole armor are God. That ye may be able to stand against the wiles of the devil. For we wrestle not against flesh and blood, but against principalities, against power, against the rulers of the darkness of this world, against spiritual wickedness in high places, wherefore take unto you the whole armor of God, that ye may be able to withstand in the evil day, and having done all, to stand. Stand therefore, having your loins girt about with truth, and having on The Breastplate of Righteousness; and your feet shod with the preparation of the Gospel of Peace. And above all, taking the Shield of Faith, wherewith ye shall be able to quench all the fiery darts of the wicked. And take the Helmet of Salvation and the Sword of the Spirit, which is The Word of God. Praying always with all prayer and supplication in the Spirit, and watching thereunto with all perseverance and supplication for all Saints."

Jesus trained and taught His disciples on how to properly evangelize and that is why I have, by the Spirit of the Lord, given you your start-up instructions along with godly wisdom concerning street preaching and street witnessing. I have done this to help assist you in becoming some of God's anointed and effective street witnesses for His glory. Amen.

It is time to go out and reap the harvest of souls for the Lord and always remember to acknowledge Him before you and your witness team venture out to witness. Also, remember, you are not a solo artist, you are a team working together and collaborating to bring souls into the kingdom of God, even if the team consists of you and the Holy Spirit and the angels! Be alert, be quick and sober, spiritually speaking, because the enemy is seeking to devour you, especially as you are out ministering to people and snatching them from the grips of death and hell. Know that the power of the Holy Ghost is in you to perform and complete God's assignment. It is your time! Let's get started!

Chapter Two: God's Plan of Salvation

How then can you and I become effective witnesses for the Lord Jesus Christ? I'm glad you asked! First and foremost, arm yourself with the Word of the Kingdom. Here are several essential scriptures that you should aim to commit to memory over time or put placeholders/markings in your Bible, as these are the foundational scriptures to minister to most people.

St. John 3: 17-18

"For God sent not His Son into the world to condemn the world; but that the world through Him might be saved. He that believeth on Him is not condemned; but he that believeth not is condemned already, because he hath not believed in the name of the only begotten Son of God."

St. Luke 19: 9-10

"And Jesus said unto him, this day is salvation come to this house, forsomuch as He also is a son of Abraham. For the Son of man is come to seek and to save that which was lost."

St. Matthew 9: 12-13

"But when Jesus heard that, he said unto them, they that be whole need not a physician, but they that are sick. But go ye and learn what that meaneth, I will have mercy, and not sacrifice: For I am not come to call the righteous, but sinners to repentance."

Romans 3: 23

"For all have sinned, and come short of the glory of God."

St. John 10: 10

"The thief cometh not, but for to steal, and to kill, and to destroy; I am come that they might have life, and that they might have it more abundantly."

St. Matthew 11: 28-30

"Come unto Me, all ye that labour and are heavy laden, and I will give you rest. Take My yoke upon you, and learn of Me, for I am meek and lowly in heart, and ye shall find rest unto your souls. For My yoke is easy, and My burden is light."

Jeremiah 33: 3

"Call unto Me, and I will answer thee, and show thee great and mighty things, which thou knowest not."

Jeremiah 31: 3

The Lord hath appeared of old unto me, saying, "Ye, I have loved thee with an everlasting love; Therefore, with loving-kindness have I drawn thee."

St. John 3: 16

"For God so loved the world that He gave his only begotten Son, that whosoever believeth in Him should not perish, but have everlasting life."

St. John 6: 37-40

"All that the Father giveth Me shall come to Me, and him that cometh to Me I will in no way cast out! And this is the will of Him that sent Me. That everyone which seeth the Son, and believeth on Him, may have everlasting life; and I will raise Him up at the last day."

A Call to Redemption

St. John 1: 11-14

"He came unto His own, and His own received Him not. But as many as received Him, to them gave He power to become the sons of God, even to them that believe on His name; which were born, not of blood, nor of the will of the flesh, nor of the will of man, but of God. And the Word was made flesh, and dwelt among us, and we beheld His glory, the glory as of the only begotten of the Father. Full of grace and truth."

Isaiah 55: 6-7

"Seek ye The Lord while He may be found, call ye upon Him while He is near; Let the wicked forsake his way, and the unrighteous man his thoughts; and let him return unto The Lord, and he will have mercy upon him, and to our God, for He will abundantly pardon."

Revelations 21: 5

And He that sat upon the throne said, "Behold, I make all things new!"

Revelations 3: 20-22

"Behold, I stand at the door, and knock; If any man hears My voice, and open the door, I will come in to him, and will sit with him, and he with Me. To him that overcometh will I grant to sit with Me in My throne, even as I also overcame, and am set down with My Father in His throne? He that hath an ear, let him hear what the Spirit said unto the churches."

Revelations 1: 18

"I am He that liveth, and was dead; and, behold, I am alive for evermore, Amen; and have the keys of hell and of death."

St. John 3: 35-36

"The Father love the Son, and hath given all things into His hand. He that believeth on the Son hath everlasting life; and he that believeth not the son shall not see life; but the wrath of God abideth on him."

St. John 3: 3

Jesus answered and said, "Unto him, verily, I say unto thee, except a man be born again, he cannot see the Kingdom of God."

Romans 6: 23

"For the wages of sin is death; but the gift of God is eternal life through Jesus Christ our Lord."

Romans 5: 8

"But God commandeth His love toward us, in that, while we were yet sinners, Christ died for us."

Psalms 51: 10

"Create in me a clean heart, Oh God; and renew a right spirit within me."

Psalms 46: 1

"God is our refuge and strength; a very present to help in trouble."

1 Peter 4: 16-19

"Yet if any man suffer as a Christian, let him not be ashamed, but let him glorify God on this behalf. For the time is come that judgment must begin at the house of God. And if it first begin at us, what shall the end be of them that obey not the gospel of God? And if the righteous scarcely be saved, where shall the ungodly and the sinner appear? Wherefore let them that suffer according to the will of God commit the keeping of their souls to Him in well doing, as unto a faithful creator."

Chapter Three: Repent and Turn to the Lord!

One of the major components to salvation is confessing one's sins and receiving forgiveness. Confessing involves repenting to the Lord Jesus of all sins that have been committed. Repenting is not the act of being sorry for what you've done. To repent mean to completely turn away from the behavior that caused you to sin.

Here are several scriptures on the topic of repentance and forgiveness.

1 Peter 2: 21-22

"For even hereunto were ye called, because Christ also suffered for us, leaving us an example, that ye should follow His steps. Who did no sin, neither was guile found in his mouth."

1 Peter 3: 18

"For Christ also hath once suffered for sins, the just for the unjust, that He might bring to us to God, being put to death in the flesh, but quickened by the Spirit."

Ephesians 2: 1-5

"And you hath He quickened, who were dead in trespasses and sins; wherein in time past ye walked according to the course of this world, according to the prince of the power of the air. The spirit that now worketh in the children of disobedience; among whom also we all had our conversation in time past in the lusts of our flesh, fulfilling the desires of the flesh and of the mind; and were by the nature the children of wrath, even as others. But God, who is rich in mercy, for His great love wherewith He loved us. Even when we were dead in sins, hath quickened us together with Christ, by grace ye are saved."

1 John: 8-9

"If we say that we have no sin we deceive ourselves, and the truth is not in us. If we confess our sins, He is faithful and just to forgive us of our sins. And to cleanse us from all unrighteousness."

Isaiah 1: 18

"Come now, and let us reason together, saith The Lord; though your sins be as scarlet, they shall be as white as snow, though they be red like crimson, they shall be as wool."

Joshua 24: 15

"And if it seem evil unto you to serve The Lord, choose you this day whom ye will serve; whether the gods which your fathers served that were on the other side of the floor, or the gods of the Amorites, in whose land ye dwell; but as for me and my house, we will serve The Lord."

Deuteronomy 30: 19

"I call Heaven and earth to record this day against you, that I have set before you life and death, blessing and cursing; therefore choose life, that both thou and thy seed may live."

Isaiah 5: 13-14

"Therefore my people are gone into captivity, because they have no knowledge; and their honorable men are famished, and their multitude dried up with thirst. Therefore hell hath enlarged herself, and opened her mouth without measure; and their glory, and their multitude, and their pomp, and he that rejoiceth, shall descend into it."

St. John 3: 3-7

"Jesus answered and said unto him, verily, verily, I say unto Thee, except a man be born again, he cannot see the Kingdom of God. Nicodemus saith unto him, how can a man be born when he is old? Can he enter the second time into his mother's womb, and be born? Jesus answered, verily, verily, I say unto Thee, except a man be born of water and of the spirit, he cannot enter into the Kingdom of God. That which is born of the flesh is flesh; and that which is born of the spirit is spirit. Marvel not that I said unto Thee, ye must be born again."

Psalm 51: 1-4

"Have mercy upon me, O God, according unto the multitude of Thy tender mercies blot out my transgression. Wash me thoroughly from mine iniquity, and cleanse me from my sin. For I acknowledge my transgressions; and my sin is ever before me. Against Thee, Thee only, have I sinned, and done this evil in Thy sight; that thou mightiest be justified when thou speakest, and be clear when thou judgest."

Psalm 51: 10-13

"Create in me a clean heart, O God; and renew a right spirit within me. Cast me not away from thy presence; and take not thy Holy Spirit from me. Restore unto me the joy of thy salvation; and uphold me with Thy free Spirit. Then will I teach transgressors thy ways. And sinners shall be converted unto Thee."

Ezekiel 36: 25-28

"Then will I sprinkle clean water upon you, and ye shall be clean; from all your filthiness, and from all your idols, will I cleanse you. A new heart also will I give you, and a new spirit will I put within you; and I will take away the stony heart out of your flesh, and I will give you a heart of flesh. And I will put my spirit within you, and cause you to walk in my statutes, and ye shall keep my judgements, and do them. And ye shall dwell in the land that I gave to your fathers; and ye shall be My people, and I will be your God."

Jeremiah 17: 9-10

"The heart is deceitful above all things, and desperately wicked; who can know it? I, The Lord, search the heart, I try the reins, even to give every man according to his ways, and according to the fruit of his doings."

Jeremiah 14: 20

"We acknowledge, O Lord, our wickedness, and the iniquity of our fathers; for we have sinned against Thee."

Jeremiah 10: 23-24

"O Lord, I know that the way of man is not himself; it is not in man that walketh to direct his steps. O Lord, correct me, but with judgement; not in Thine anger, lest Thou bring me to nothing."

Isaiah 53: 6

"All we like sheep have gone astray; we have turned everyone to his own way; and The Lord hath laid on Him the iniquity of us all."

Romans 10: 8-10

"But what saith it? The Word is nigh thee, even in thy mouth, and in thy heart; that is, the Word off faith, which we preach. That if thou shalt confess with thy mouth the Lord Jesus, and shalt believe in thine heart that God hath raised Him from the dead, thou shalt be saved. For with the heart of man believeth unto righteousness; and with the mouth confession is made unto salvation."

Romans 10: 13

"For whosoever shall call upon the name of The Lord shall be saved."

Romans 10: 17

"So then faith cometh by hearing, and hearing by the Word of God."

Ezekiel 3: 18-19

"When I say unto the wicked, Thou shalt surely die; and Thou givest him not warning, nor speakest to warn the wicked from his wicked way, to save his life; the same wicked man shall die in his iniquity; but his blood will I require at thine hand. Yet if Thou warn the wicked, and he turn not from his wickedness, nor from his wicked way, he shall die in his iniquity; but thou hast delivered thy soul."

Isaiah 64: 6

"But we are all as an unclean thing, and all our righteousness are as filthy rags, and we all do fade as a leaf, and out iniquities, like the wind, have taken us away."

Jeremiah 16: 17

"For mine eyes are upon all their ways, they are not hid from My face, neither is their iniquity hid from mine eyes."

Jeremiah 23: 23-24

"Am I a God at hand, saith The Lord, and not a God afar off? Can any hide himself in secret places that I shall not see him? Saith The Lord. Do not I fill Heaven and earth? Saith The Lord."

St. Matthew 7: 20

"Wherefore by their fruits ye shall know them."

1 Corinthians 15: 3-4

"For I delivered unto you first of all that which I also received, how that Christ died for our sins according to the scriptures; and that He was buried, and that He rose again the third day according to the scriptures."

Dorothy A. Nelson

St. John 6: 35-40

"...I am the bread of life; he that cometh to Me shall never hunger; and he that believeth on Me shall never thirst. But I say unto you, that ye also have seen Me, and believe not. All that the Father giveth Me shall come to Me, and Him that cometh to Me I will in no wise cast out. For I came down from Heaven, not to do Mine own will, but the will of Him that sent Me. And this is the Father's will which hath sent Me, that of all which He hath given Me I should lose nothing, but should raise it up again at the last day. And this is the will of Him that sent Me that every one which seeth the Son, and believeth on Him, may have everlasting life; and I will raise him up at the day."

St. John 6: 44-51

"No man can come to Me, except the Father which hath sent Me draw him; and I will raise him up at the last day. It is written in the prophets, and they shall be all taught of God. Every man therefore that hath heard, and hath learned of the Father, cometh unto Me. Not that any man hath seen the Father, save he which is of God, he hath seen the Father. Verily, verily, I say unto you, He that believeth on Me hath everlasting life. I am that bread of life! Your Fathers did eat manna in the wilderness, and are dead. This is the bread which cometh down from Heaven, that a man may eat thereof, and not die. I am the living bread which came down from Heaven; if any man eat of this bread, he shall live forever, and the bread that I will give is My flesh, which I will give for the life of the world."

St. John 6: 65

"...Therefore said I unto you, that no man can come unto Me except it were given unto him of My Father."

St. John 14: 6

"...I am the Way, the Truth, and the Life; no man cometh unto the Father, but by Me!"

Ephesians 1: 4-7

"According as he hath chosen us in Him before the foundation of the world. That we should be holy and without blame before Him in live. Having predestinated us unto the adoption of children by Jesus Christ to Himself, according to the good pleasure of His will. To the praise of His glory of His grace, wherein He hath made us accepted in His beloved. In whom we have redemption through His blood, the forgiveness of sin, according to the riches of His glory!"

Ephesians 2: 12-13

"That at the time ye were without Christ, being aliens from the Commonwealth of Israel, and strangers from the Covenants of Promise, having no hope, and without God in the world. But now in Christ Jesus ye who sometime were far off are made nigh by the blood of Christ."

Ephesians 2: 4-5

"But God, who is rich in mercy, for his great love wherewith He loved us. Even when we were dead in sins, hath quickened us together with Christ, by grace ye are saved."

St. John 1: 1-4

"In the beginning was the Word, (Jesus) and The Word was with God, and The Word was God. The same was in the beginning with God. All things were made by Him; and without Him was not anything made that was made. In Him was life; and the life was the light of men."

Romans 3: 23-24

"For all have sinned, and come short of the glory of God; being justified freely by His grace through the redemption that is Christ Jesus."

Romans 3: 10

"As it is written, there is none righteous, no not one."

Romans 10: 13-14

"For whosoever shall call upon the name of The Lord shall be saved. How then shall they call on Him in whom they have not believed? And how shall they believe in Him of whom they have not heard? And how shall they hear without a preacher?"

1 Timothy 2: 3-6

"For this is good and acceptable in the sight of God our Savior; who will have all men to be saved, and to come unto the knowledge of the truth. For there is one God, and one Mediator between God and men, the man Christ Jesus; who gave Himself a ransom for all, to be testified in due time."

Isaiah 59: 1-2

"Behold, The Lord's hand is not shortened, that it cannot save; neither His ear heavy. That it cannot hear; but your iniquities have separated between you and your God, and your sins have hid His face from you that He will not hear."

St. Matthew 9: 13

"But go ye and learn what the meaneth, I will have mercy, and not sacrifice; for I am not come to call the righteous, but sinners to repentance."

Acts 3: 19

"Repent ye therefore, and be converted, that your sins may be blotted out, when the times of refreshing shall come from the presence of The Lord."

Acts 4: 12

"Neither is there salvation in any other, for there is none other name under Heaven given among men, where by we must be saved."

Ezekiel 18: 31-32

"Cast away from you all your transgressions, whereby ye have transgressed; and make you a new heart and a new spirit; for why will ye die, o house of Israel? For I have no pleasure in the death of him that dieth, saith The Lord God; wherefore turn yourselves, and live ye."

St. Mark 1: 15

"The time is fulfilled, and the Kingdom of God is at hand; Repent Ye, and believe the Gospel."

St. Luke 13: 5

"I tell you, nay; but, except ye repent, ye shall all likewise perish."

St. Luke 15: 7

"I say unto you, that likewise joy shall be in Heaven over one sinner that repenteth, more than over ninety and nine just person, which need no repentance."

Romans 5: 8-19

"But God commendeth His love toward us, in that, while we were yet sinners, Christ died for us. Much more then, being now justified by His blood, we shall be saved from wrath through Him. For it, when we were enemies, we were reconciled to God by, the death of His Son, much more, being reconciled, we shall be saved by His life. And not only so, but we also joy in God through Our Lord Jesus Christ, by whom we have now received the atonement. Wherefore, as by one man sin entered into the world, and death by sin; and so death passed upon all men, for that all have sinned; for until the law sin was in the world; but sin is not imputed when there is no law. Nevertheless, death reigned from Adam to Moses, even over them that hath not sinned after the similitude of Adam's transgression, who is the figure of him that was to come. But not as the offense, so also is the free gift, for if through the offense of one many be dead, much more the grace of God, and the gift by grace, which is by one man, Jesus Christ, hath abounded unto many. And not as it was by one that sinned, so is the gift; for the judgement was by one to condemnation, but the free gift is of many offenses unto justification. For if by one man's offense death reigned by one; much more they which receive abundance of grace and of the gift of righteousness shall reign in life. Therefore as by the offense of one judgement came upon all men to condemnation; even so by the righteousness of one the free gift came upon all men unto justification of life. For as by one man's disobedience many were made sinners, so by the obedience of One shall many be made righteous."

Hebrews 9: 11-12

"But Christ being come a high priest of good things to come, by a great and more perfect tabernacle. Not made with hands, that is to say, not of this building; neither by the blood of goats and calves, but by His own blood He entered into once in the holy place, having obtained eternal redemption for us."

Hebrews 9: 27-28

"And as it is appointed unto me once to die, but after this the judgment. So Christ was once offered to bear the sins of many; and unto them that look for Him shall He appear the second time without sin unto salvation."

Hebrews 11: 6

"But without faith it is impossible to please Him, for He that cometh to God must believe that He is, and that He is a rewarded of them that diligently seek Him."

1 Peter 3: 18

"For Christ also hath once suffered for sins, the just for the unjust, that He might bring us to God, being put to death in the flesh, but quickened by the Spirit."

1 John 1: 8-9

"If we say that we have no sin, we deceive ourselves, and the truth is not in us. If we confess our sins, He is faithful and just to forgive us our sins, and to cleanse us from all unrighteousness."

1 John 2: 1-2

"My little children, these things write I unto you, that ye sin not, and if any man sin, we have an advocate with the Father, Jesus Christ the righteous; and He is the propitiation for our sins; and not for ours only, but also for the sins of the whole world!"

1 John 3: 7-9

"Little children, let no man deceive you; he that doeth righteousness is righteous, even as he is righteous. He that committeth sin is of the devil; for the devil sinneth from the beginning. For this purpose the Son of God was manifested, that He might destroy the works of the devil. Whosoever is born of God doth not commit sin; for his seed remaineth in him; and he cannot sin, because he is born of God."

1 John 5: 4-6

"For whatsoever is born of God overcometh the world; and this is the victory that overcometh the world, even our faith. Who is he that overcometh the world, but he that believeth that Jesus is the Son of God? This is he that came by water and blood, even Jesus Christ; not by water only, but by water and blood. And it is the Spirit that beareth witness, because the Spirit is Truth."

Philippians 2: 6-11

"Who, being in the form of God, thought it not robbery to be equal with God; But made Himself of no reputation, and took upon Him the form of a servant, and was made in the likeness of man; and being found in fashion as a man, He humbled Himself, even the death of the cross. Wherefore God also hath highly exalted Him, and given Him a name which is above every name; That at the name of Jesus every knee should bow, of things in Heaven, and things in earth, and things under the earth. And that every tongue should confess that Jesus Christ is Lord, to the glory of God the Father."

Galatians 6: 7-8

"Be not deceived; God is not mocked; for whatsoever a man soweth, that shall he also reap. For he that soweth to his flesh shall of the flesh reap corruption; but he that soweth to the Spirit shall of the Spirit reap life everlasting."

Titus 2: 11-12

"For the grace of God that bringeth salvation hath appeared to all men. Teaching us that denying ungodliness and worldly lust, we should live soberly, righteously, and Godly, in this present world."

Titus 3: 5

"Not by works of righteousness which we have done. But according to His mercy He saved us, by the washing of regeneration, and renewing of the Holy Ghost."

Hebrews 2: 9

"But we see Jesus, who was made a little lower than the Angels for the suffering of death, crowned with glory and honour; that he by the grace of God should taste death for every man."

Hebrews 2: 3

"How shall we escape, if we neglect so great salvation; which at the first began to be spoken by The Lord, and was confirmed unto us by them that hear him?"

Hebrews 12: 2

"Looking unto Jesus the Author and Finisher of our faith; who for the joy that was set before Him endured the cross, despising the shame, and is set down at the right hand of the throne of God."

Hebrews 12: 14

"Follow peace with all men, and holiness, without which no man shall see The Lord."

James 4: 17

"Therefore to him that knoweth to do good, and doeth it not, to him it is sin."

Galatians 4: 4-5

"But when the fullness of the time was come, God sent forth His Son made of a woman, made under the law, to redeem them that were under the law, that we might receive the adoption of sons."

Galatians 4: 9

"But now, after that ye have known God, or rather are known of God, how turn ye again to the weak and beggarly elements, whereunto ye desire again to be in bondage?"

1 Corinthians 15: 22

"For as in Adam all die, even so in Christ shall all be made alive."

2 Corinthians 5: 17

"Therefore if any man be in Christ, he is a new creature; old things are passed away; behold, all things are become new."

2 Corinthians 5: 21

"For He hath made Him to be sin for us, who knew no sin, that we might be made the righteousness of God in Him."

2 Corinthians 7: 10

"For Godly sorrow worketh repentance to salvation not to be repented of; but the sorrow of the world worketh death."

Colossians 2: 9

"For in Him dwelleth all the fullness of the God head bodily."

Colossians 2: 14-15

"Blotting out the handwriting of ordinances that was against us, which was contrary to us, and took it out of the way, nailing it to the cross. And having spoiled principalities and powers, he made a shew of them openly, triumphing over them in it."

Isaiah 59: 1-2

"Behold, The Lord's hand is not shortened, that it cannot save, neither his ear heavy, that it cannot hear; But your iniquities have separated between you and your God. And your sins have hid his face from you that he will not hear."

My fellow laborers in the gospel, I pray that this salvation guide will be a tremendous blessing to you and will assist you in your ministry, as you will be fully prepared to go out into the streets and win souls to bring into the Kingdom of God! Amen.

I carefully composed all the main scriptures that are utilized in leading those to salvation. I pray that you will become familiar with these scriptures and that they will help you and your ministry team. I feel it is vital to have a reference of salvation scriptures which will guide you through the process in leading souls to the Lord Jesus Christ.

Dorothy A. Nelson

Please read the booklet like you would read your Bible. It will help you throughout your ministry. Always keep this on hand as your personal reference to soul-winning! May God bless you and your ministry and may this booklet become your friend in your Kingdom assignment in soul witnessing!

Salvation Confession

1 John 1: 9

"Say, if we confess our sins, he is faithful and just to forgive us our sins, and to cleanse us from all unrighteousness." Amen.

Now repeat these words:

"Lord Jesus, I believe that You are the Son of God and that You came into the world to die for my sins. And I believe that you rose again on the third day. Jesus come into my heart and be my Lord and Savior. I accept You and Your Word now, according to Romans 10:9-10 which says, "That is thou shalt confess with thy mouth the Lord Jesus, and shalt believe in thine heart that God hath raised him from the dead, thou shalt be saved. For with the heart man believeth unto righteousness; and with the mouth confession is made unto salvation."

Thank you Jesus for Your death and resurrection. I am saved now, according to my confession of faith in the living Savior. Hallelujah! I'm saved! Thank you Lord!

Now that you have received Jesus as your Savior, tell somebody about it, because your confession of faith is so very important! Also, be ready to recommend a good Bible believing church that teaches and preaches the Gospel of the Kingdom so that they may continue to grow in their faith and receive the sincere milk of The Word. Get them connected with a body of believers!

Now that they are saved there is one more step and this final step is that of the infilling of the Holy Spirit, according to St. John 7 :37-38:

"...If any man thirst, let him come unto me, and drink. He that believeth on me, as the scripture hath said, out of his belly shall flow rivers of living water, and that is the Holy Spirit."

Now you may ask the Lord Jesus to fill you with his Holy Spirit, just by asking and receiving it by faith. Let's look at Acts 1:8 and Acts 19:2:

"But ye shall receive power, after that the Holy Spirit (Ghost) is come upon you; and ye shall be witnesses unto me both in Jerusalem, and in all Judea, and in Samaria, and unto the uttermost part of the Earth."

"He said unto them, have ye received the Holy Ghost since ye believed? And they said unto him, we have not so much as

heard whether there be any Holy Ghost. And when Paul had laid his hands upon them, the Holy Ghost came on them; and they spake with tongues, and prophesied."

As you can now see, this gift is for you to help you in your Christian walk. It will give you that extra power that you will need to live and walk in this new life. He, the Holy Spirit, is a Helper, a Keeper and a Comforter in your hours of need. Receive Him now by asking Him to fill you! Let the rivers of living water flow out of you right now! Thank Him, Jesus, for filling you with His Spirit! Read St. John 14 completely. It will truly help you with understanding and enlightenment as to who He is and why we need Him! Amen.

About the Author

Apostle Dorothy A. Nelson, along with her husband Pastor David Nelson, are the pastors of New Destiny of Faith Kingdom Ministry. She has been preaching the Gospel for over 30 years and is going stronger than ever to help spread the Gospel of the Kingdom of God throughout the world. God continues to bless her to flow in the psalmist, prophetic and healing anointing with authenticity, accuracy and signs, wonders and miracles to follow the preached Word of God.

God has graced Apostle Nelson to be the author of several books including: The Healing Wings of God, Don't Let the Devil Steal Your Confession and God's Prophetic Word to the Church. Other books are in the process of being re-released in its second edition.

She pursued a bachelor's degree in Sociology and Psychology at Indiana University Northwest. She also obtained certification in Biblical Counseling. As a former house supervisor for mentally challenged patients, she was able to utilize her God-given gifts to provide training, counseling and teaching to her clients.

Apostle and Pastor Nelson's vision is to continue to establish supernatural churches that are actively flowing in every facet and realm of the Spirit. The primary focuses of the ministry are wholeness to the family manifesting the glory of God through the preached Word of God. Being supernaturally cancer free for 18 years, the Lord has given her a special grace, anointing and care for those being challenged in their physical bodies.

In addition to ministering to the spiritual needs of His people, God has given Apostle Nelson a vision to care for the natural needs as well. She is in the process of establishing a shopping plaza and counseling center.

Apostle Nelson has been married to Pastor David Nelson for over 38 years. Together they have six children, Dorothy Renee, Martin, David, Charity, Samuel and Ola, and twenty two grandchildren.

Dorothy A. Nelson

LET'S STAY CONNECTED!

Go to www.dorothynelson.org to keep updated on upcoming events and other information.

Follow Pastor Dorothy on:
Facebook: www.facebook.com/Dorothy.nelson.18
Twitter: @ApostleDorothy

Join her every Wednesday night from 6:15pm –7:15pm EST on WLLV radio 1240 AM and Sunday morning from 11:30am-12pm on WLOU radio 104.7 FM.

If you have a prayer request or praise report, feel free to email us: info@dorothynelson.org

New Destiny Ministry Intl'
P.O Box 16788
Louisville, KY 40256

Other Books by Dorothy A. Nelson
"God Prophetic Message to the Church"
"Stand"
"Don't Let the Devil Steal your Confession"
"God's Biblical Perspective on Christian Counseling"
"Scriptures that Bring Healing" (Book and CD pack)
"The Road to Salvation" (Coming Soon)

A Call to Redemption

www.ingramcontent.com/pod-product-compliance
Lightning Source LLC
Chambersburg PA
CBHW070549300426
44113CB00011B/1843